Why did the boy give his girlfriend a baseball field?
He wanted to give her the biggest diamond in town.

What does a Valentine envelope say when you lick it?
Nothing. It shuts up.

What did the Valentine's card say to the stamp?
Stick with me and we'll go places!

For Grandmother and Heidi,
two sweethearts who share their love year 'round.
Connie & Peter Roop

To my Malcolm
Katy Keck Arnsteen

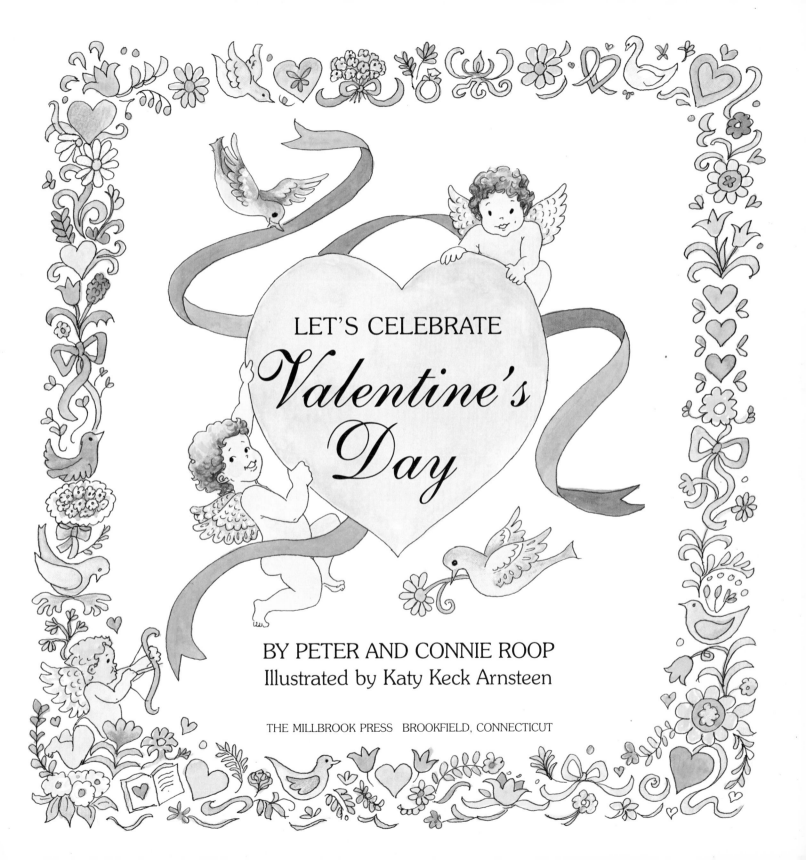

LET'S CELEBRATE

Valentine's
Day

BY PETER AND CONNIE ROOP

Illustrated by Katy Keck Arnsteen

THE MILLBROOK PRESS   BROOKFIELD, CONNECTICUT

Library of Congress Cataloging-in-Publication Data
Roop, Peter.
Let's celebrate Valentine's Day / by Peter and Connie Roop; illustrated by Katy Keck Arnsteen.
p.   cm.
Summary: Describes some history and customs connected with St. Valentine's day and presents jokes, riddles, activities, and recipes to help celebrate this holiday.
ISBN 0-7613-0972-1 (lib. bdg.) . —ISBN 0-7613-0428-2 (trade pbk.)
1. Valentine's Day–Juvenile literature. [1. Valentine's Day.] I. Roop, Connie.
II. Arnsteen, Katy Keck, ill. III. Title.
GT4925.R66   1999
394.2618—dc21   98-13971   CIP   AC

Published by The Millbrook Press, Inc.
2 Old New Milford Road
Brookfield, CT 06804

You have just signed your name 25 times on 25 cards. But you are excited. Today you will get lots and lots of cards. Some will have funny sayings on them. Some will say, "Be Mine!" You might even get one that says "I love you!" What day is it? Valentine's Day!

Who Was Valentine?

No one is quite sure who the real Valentine was, but many stories have been told. One is about a priest named Valentine.

A Roman emperor had decided that no young men could get married. Why? Because he wanted them for his army. Valentine thought the emperor was wrong, so he secretly married many young men and women. When the emperor found out, he had Valentine arrested, put in jail, and, on February 14, 269 A.D., put to death.

A story about another Valentine takes place when he was in jail for disobeying the emperor. His jailer had a blind daughter. Valentine helped her to see again. Then he fell in love with her and wrote her love letters signed "From your Valentine."

Today, on February 14, we still sign Valentine's Day cards "From your Valentine."

What animal loves Valentine's Day?

A deer.

What animal loves wet Valentine's Day cards?

A reindeer.

What kinds of ships do friends sail in?

Friendships.

What did one chocolate heart say to the other?

Will you be my sweet-heart?

For Dracula and his girlfriend, it was love at first bite.

Why Is Valentine's Day on February 14?

Valentine's Day is on February 14 to remember the day Valentine died.

February 14 was also the beginning of a special Roman festival called Lupercalia. This celebration was exciting for young Roman boys and girls because there was lots of singing and dancing. Before the festival began, the girls put their names into a jar. Then each boy reached in to select one name. That girl would be his partner for the Lupercalia celebrations.

One exciting part of Lupercalia was when two boys swinging strings made from goatskins ran through crowds of girls. If the strings touched a girl, it meant that she would have a good year and she would have healthy children when she grew up. The goatskin strings were called *februa*, which means to make clean. From the word *februa* we get the name of our month February, the month in which Valentine's Day is celebrated!

Later the festival was changed to honor the memory of St. Valentine. But it still remained a spring holiday when people expressed their affection for one another.

A kiss on Valentine's Day brings good luck all year.

Throughout history there have been eight St. Valentines. Three of them had special feast days in their honor.

Madame Royale, a French princess, loved Valentine's Day so much that she named her palace "The Valentine."

Who Celebrates Valentine's Day?

Valentine's Day has been celebrated in England for more than 500 years. When the Romans invaded Britain they brought the holiday with them. Today, girls and boys get pennies or candy for singing songs. In Italy people have a St. Valentine's Day feast. They sing romantic songs, recite love poems, and just enjoy each other's company. Valentine cards are sent in Germany, Spain, Austria, and other countries in Europe. Canada and America, however, celebrate Valentine's Day the most.

Valentine's Day is a popular day to get married.

When a man asked a woman to marry him, he asked for her hand in marriage. The hand (and later gloves, too) became symbols of love.

Girls born on Valentine's Day are sometimes named Valerie.

If you are awakened by a kiss on Valentine's Day, you will have good luck.

Some people believe that the first person you see on February 14 will be your Valentine.

Long ago women believed that magic spells and charms would tell them who their husbands would be.

How Did People Celebrate Valentine's Day Long Ago?

Long ago it was a tradition to bake a big cake on Valentine's Day. Inside the cake were different Valentine tokens. If your piece of cake had a ring in it, it meant you would get married soon. If a coin was in your piece, it meant you would soon be rich. If you got a tiny red mitten, it meant your girlfriend did not like you anymore.

Heart-shaped cookies and candy were served at many Valentine parties. Boys and girls played Drop the Handkerchief. This is like Duck, Duck, Goose, except that if a boy catches a girl he gets to kiss her!

In England, a girl would pin four bay leaves to her pillow. If she dreamed of a boy that night, she would soon marry him. English boys and girls also wrote their names on small pieces of paper. They rolled the papers into balls and covered them with clay. When the clay balls were dropped into water, the clay broke apart, and the papers floated to the surface. The first name they could read would tell them who they were going to marry.

In Germany, girls would write the names of boys on pieces of paper. They would stick them onto onions and place the onions in a warm corner by a fireplace. The first onion to sprout told the girls who they would marry.

If a German boy really loved a girl, he gave her a pair of gloves. If she kept them, it meant she agreed to marry him.

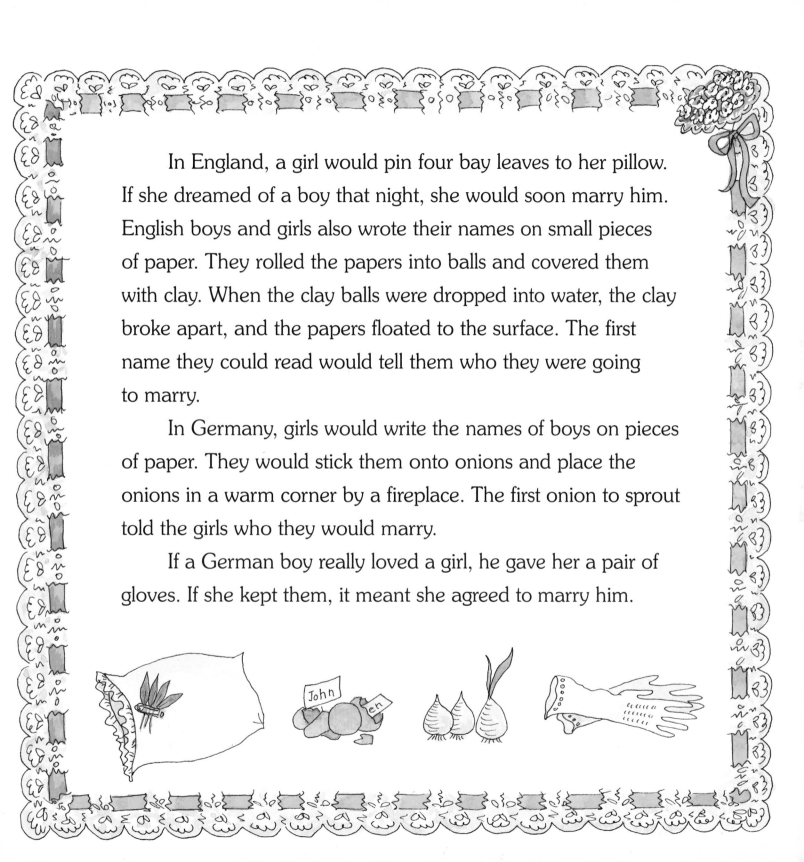

Why Is Cupid a Valentine Symbol?

Have you ever seen a picture of a chubby little boy with wings on his back and a bow and arrow in his hands? He's Cupid, one of our most popular Valentine's Day symbols.

The story of Cupid comes from long ago. He was a god of the Romans, the same people who put the first Valentine to death. Cupid's mother was Venus, the goddess of love. Cupid was a happy god, and he liked to make others happy, too. He would go around shooting gold-tipped arrows into the hearts of unsuspecting people. As soon as the arrow struck, the people fell in love.

Why was Cupid locked up in jail?

He was caught stealing hearts.

What did the light say to the room?

I've taken a shine to you.

In England, pretend money called "love money" was given on Valentine's Day. Some of the love money looked so real that people spent it. The English government soon outlawed it.

The biggest kiss ever made by Hershey weighed 400 pounds.

One-fifth of the world's chocolate and cocoa is eaten by Americans.

The Aztec emperor Montezuma drank fifty servings of cocoa each day. He drank from a gold goblet.

Almost seven billion candy hearts are sold each Valentine's Day.

What does a kiss taste like?

Chocolate!

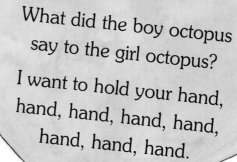

What did the boy octopus say to the girl octopus?

I want to hold your hand, hand, hand, hand, hand, hand, hand, hand.

Why Are Birds and Flowers Symbols For Valentine's Day?

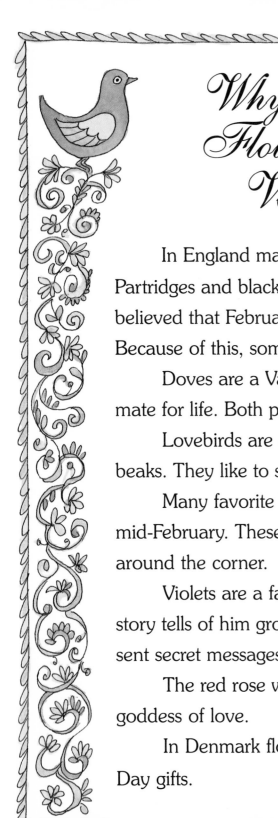

In England many birds returned from the south in February. Partridges and blackbirds built their nests in mid-February. It was believed that February 14 was the day that birds picked their mates. Because of this, some birds have become Valentine's Day symbols.

Doves are a Valentine's symbol of loyalty and love. Doves mate for life. Both parents take care of their babies.

Lovebirds are colorful parrots from Africa. Most have red beaks. They like to sit closely together in pairs.

Many favorite Valentine flowers are just beginning to bloom in mid-February. These flowers remind people that spring is just around the corner.

Violets are a favorite Valentine flower. Another St. Valentine story tells of him growing violets in the window of his jail cell. He sent secret messages to friends with the blossoms.

The red rose was the favorite flower of Venus, the Roman goddess of love.

In Denmark flowers called snowdrops are popular Valentine's Day gifts.

Say it with a flower . . .

Red roses mean love.

Yellow roses mean friendship.

Pink roses mean friendship or sweetheart.

Red carnations mean admiration.

White carnations mean pure love.

Red chrysanthemums mean I love you.

Forget-me-nots mean true love.

Primrose means young love.

Larkspur means an open heart.

What did the insect
say to the flower?

Will you bee
my Valentine?

Which flowers like to kiss
on Valentine's Day?

Tulips.

What did the bee
say to the flower on
Valentine's Day?

"Hi, Honey!"

Why Is Red a Valentine's Day Color?

Long ago the color red meant blood. How did it become the color of love? We know that the heart pumps blood through our bodies. At one time people also thought that the heart was the part of the body that felt love. Today, red Valentine hearts mean love.

We still connect our hearts to our feelings. Someone who is sad might be called "broken-hearted." A good feeling is "heart-warming." A mean person might be called "heartless."

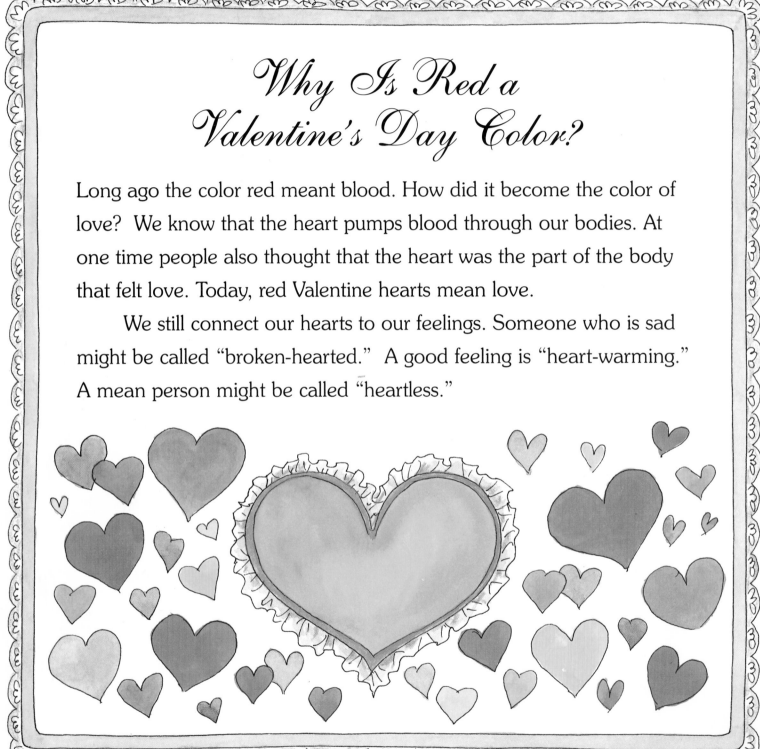

I Love You

AROUND THE WORLD

Afrikaans – *Ek het jou lief*

Arabic - *Ib'n hebbak*

Chinese - *Wo ai ni*

Danish - *Jeg elsker dig*

Dutch - *Ik hou van jou*

French - *Je t'aime*

German - *Ich liebe dich*

Hawaiian - *Aloha I'a Au Oe*

Japanese - *Kimi o ai shiteru*

Navaho - *Ayor anosh'ni*

Polish - *Kocham cie*

Portuguese - *Amo te*

Russian - *Ya vas liubliu*

Spanish - *Te Amo*

Yiddish - *Ich libe dich*

Zulu - *Mena Tanda Wena*

I LOVE YOU!

What Were Valentine's Day Cards Like Long Ago?

According to legend, the first Valentine was sent in February 1415 by the English duke of Orleans. He sent a love letter to his wife from his jail cell in the Tower of London. The tradition of Valentine's Day cards came to America with the first settlers from England.

Of course all those cards were made by hand. Boys spent many hours making valentines for their sweethearts. So did girls. Later, Valentine's Day cards were made by machine. There were plain ones and fancy ones. Lace, ribbons, silk, velvet, feathers, and even little glass ornaments were added.

Many cards held surprises. Girls sometimes tucked in a lock of hair. A boy might give his favorite friend a card with perfume in it. Some valentines were puzzles. Others had moving parts. Braille valentines were made for the blind.

Cards were not the only tokens of affection shared on Valentine's Day. Many boys would sing or recite their Valentine verses hoping to win their Valentine's love. Girls would give boys small pieces of silk with their initials stitched on them. The boys used the silk inside their pocket watches to keep the dust out. So every time they opened the watch to check the time, they would see the initials of their Valentine.

Long ago if you got a Valentine's card in the mail you had to pay the postage. If you did not like the card you asked for your money back.

The first glitter was made from ground glass.

One billion Valentine cards are given in the United States each year.

Each year 300,000 Valentines go through Loveland, Colorado, to get a special heart stamp cancellation.

More than 100 years ago, the Chicago post office refused to deliver about 25,000 Valentine postcards because their messages were not nice. They were called "vinegar valentines."

One expensive Valentine's Day card had 3,000 pieces of lace, silk, and other decorations on it.

Teachers get the most Valentines. Children are second.

Here are some fun Valentine's Day sentiments:

Roses are red,
violets are blue,
carnations are sweet,
and so are you.
And so is he,
who sends you this,
and when we meet,
we'll have a kiss.

De liver de letter
De sooner de better
De later de letter
De madder I getter.

Plenty of love
tons of kisses
hope some day
to be your Mrs.

The Kangaroo's Courtship
Oh, will you be my wallaby?
Asked Mr. Kangaroo.
For we could find so very many
Jumping things to do.
I have a pocket two feet wide
And deep inside, my dear, you'd ride.
Oh, come and be my bouncing bride,
My Valentine, my side-by-side,
I am in love with you.

"Doubt thou the stars are fire;
Doubt that the sun doth move;
Doubt truth to be a liar;
But never doubt I love."
—*William Shakespeare*

"'Tis better to have loved and lost
Then never to have loved at all."
—*Alfred Lord Tennyson*

Valentine, Valentine, who will you be?
A yawning sloth that hangs from a tree, or a
Long-legged giraffe with big brown eyes,
Elusive elephant of enormous size,
Nattering parrot of yackety yak,
Thirsty camel with a hump on his back,
Itching monkey, bumbling old bear,
Nosy narwhal, or panda rare,
Earnest emu who cannot fly,
Smallest chickadee in the sky, or
Dandy Kangaroo who bounds so high?
All of these animals in the zoo
Yearn to be mine . . . but I'd rather have you!

Make Your Own Pop-Up Valentine's Day Cards!

You will need:

Stiff red, white, or pink
    tagboard
Glue
Paper and foil doilies
Pretty wrapping paper
Scissors

Construction paper
Scraps of lace
Crumpled wads of pink,
    white, or red tissue
    paper
Glitter

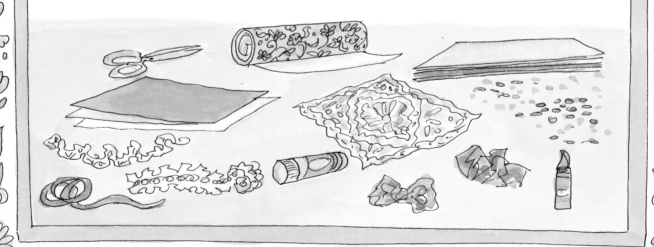

1) Cut a 6 x 10-inch pink, white, or red piece of stiff tagboard.

2) Fold in half.

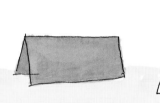

3) Arrange and paste doilies, paper and foil hearts, lace, and small wads of tissue paper on the card. The more layers of materials, the more old-fashioned your card will look. Squeeze dots of glue all over and sprinkle with glitter.

4) To make the pop-out heart, cut a 9 x ½-inch strip of the stiff tagboard. Fold it accordian-style, into a ½-inch square. Glue the bottom of one end to the middle of the inside of the card. Glue a foil or paper heart onto the other end.

Valentine Sugar Cookies

This recipe makes enough for your whole class to enjoy.

You will need:

1 cup of margarine

1 cup powdered sugar

1 cup regular sugar

½ tsp. salt

2 eggs

1 cup cooking oil

2 tsp. vanilla

1 tsp. baking soda

1 tsp. cream of tartar

5 cups sifted flour

Red sugar to sprinkle on top

Preheat the oven to 350°. Cream together the margarine, sugars, and salt.

Add the rest of the ingredients and mix well.

Drop tablespoons of dough onto an ungreased cookie sheet.

Flatten with the bottom of a glass.

You could pinch the dough into a heart shape, if you want.

Sprinkle with red sugar and bake at 350° for 10-12 minutes.